S0-BXX-655

·SUPER FACTS·
MOTORCYCLES

DAVE RICHMOND

DERRYDALE BOOKS
New York

Contents

Copyright © Grisewood & Dempsey Ltd. 1979, 1986

This 1992 edition published by Derrydale Books,
distributed by Outlet Book Company, Inc.,
a Random House Company, 225 Park Avenue South,
New York, New York 10003.

Printed and bound in Hong Kong

ISBN 0-517-07323-4
8 7 6 5 4 3 2 1

Bikes

In 1885 Gottleib Daimler designed a cumbersome two-wheeled wooden frame for his pioneering four-stroke internal combustion engine. Historians take that date as the birth of the motorcycle. Since then, more than 100 years of steady technical development has produced the huge variety of machines we have today, from docile 50 cc runabouts to giant 1300 cc superbikes.

This book tells the story of the motorcycle from its beginning to the present day. It describes how they work, and the purposes for which different machines are built. A wealth of action-packed pictures show machines on the road and in competition. Exotic dragsters, speedway bikes, motocrossers and sophisticated road racers all have something in common with models on sale throughout the world. They need skill and care on the part of the rider if they are to perform well.

Everyone who loves bikes – from the dedicated rider to the youngest enthusiast discovering the excitement of the motorcycle for the first time – will enjoy what this book has to offer.

Early Days

◄ As this French cartoon of 1818 shows, the idea of the motorcycle was once thought ridiculous.

▼ The 1885 Daimler is widely accepted as the world's first motorcycle. It had no brakes, no lights, no suspension and no gears, and with its wooden frame was incredibly slow and unwieldy.

Daimler 1885

The first machine with some of the basic features of the modern bicycle appeared in 1838 when a Scottish blacksmith, Kirkpatrick Macmillan, fitted a velocipede with a rod and treadle mechanism to drive the back wheel. This was the first time pedals were used to propel a vehicle.

Pioneer two-wheelers were clumsy and could not move at much more than walking speed. Various means were tried to make two-wheeled vehicles go faster with less effort on the part of the rider. In 1869 a steam engine was fitted to a Michaux bicycle. Other steam-driven motor bicycles soon followed.

These 'external combustion' steam engines were heavy and inefficient. Bulky fuel had to be burned outside the engine and stoking a boiler while riding must have been awkward. A solution came with the first 'internal combustion' engines, so called because they burned fuel inside the engine. Early versions such as those designed by Nicolaus Otto used coal gas. In 1876 this ingenious German engineer patented the basic four-stroke cycle

on which modern internal combustion engines work. His four-stroke stationary engine using coal gas as fuel was perfected by Gottlieb Daimler and Wilhelm Maybach. Daimler realized that a small engine fuelled by petrol could be used to power a cycle and in 1885 he built the first ever petrol-driven motorcycle. He used a wooden frame powered by a light 264 cc four-stroke engine. It spun at just 800 rpm – about one tenth of the speed of a modern engine. An improved model was ridden by a friend of Daimler for more than 3 kms 'without stopping or hesitation'.

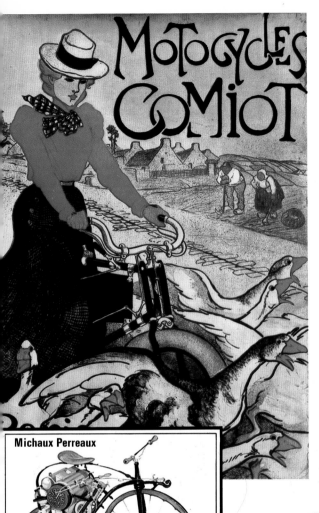

In England, Edward Butler's two-stroke petrol-driven tricycle was patented in 1887 while in France the first multi-cylinder motorcycle was constructed by Felix Millet.

All the great pioneer motorcycles were hand built by their inventors and were not sold to the public. The world's first production motorcycle appeared in 1894 when Heinrich Hildebrand and Alois Wolfmuller opened a factory in Munich, Germany, to produce their twin-cylinder four-stroke, at the rate of ten machines a day.

By the end of the 19th century factories in Switzerland, Belgium, Britain and France were producing bikes. One of the most popular was the single-cylinder Werner. With its engine placed vertically between the wheels, the 'New Werner' design was to become familiar throughout Europe.

▼ The first commercially successful motorcycle was the 1894 Hildebrand and Wolfmuller. It had a water-cooled twin-cylinder engine. Water was carried in a tank which doubled as the rear mudguard. Piston rods transmitted power to the rear wheel.

Michaux Perreaux

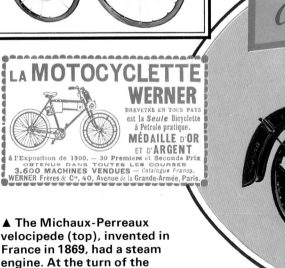

LA **MOTOCYCLETTE**
WERNER
BREVETÉE EN TOUS PAYS
est la *Seule* Bicyclette
à Pétrole pratique.
MÉDAILLE D'OR
ET D'**ARGENT**
à l'Exposition de 1900. — 30 Premiers et Seconds Prix
OBTENUS DANS TOUTES LES COURSES
3.600 MACHINES VENDUES — *Catalogue Franco.*
WERNER Frères & C¹ᵉ, 40, Avenue de la Grande-Armée, Paris.

▲ The Michaux-Perreaux velocipede (top), invented in France in 1869, had a steam engine. At the turn of the century, Werner motorcycles (below) were among the most popular in Europe.

5

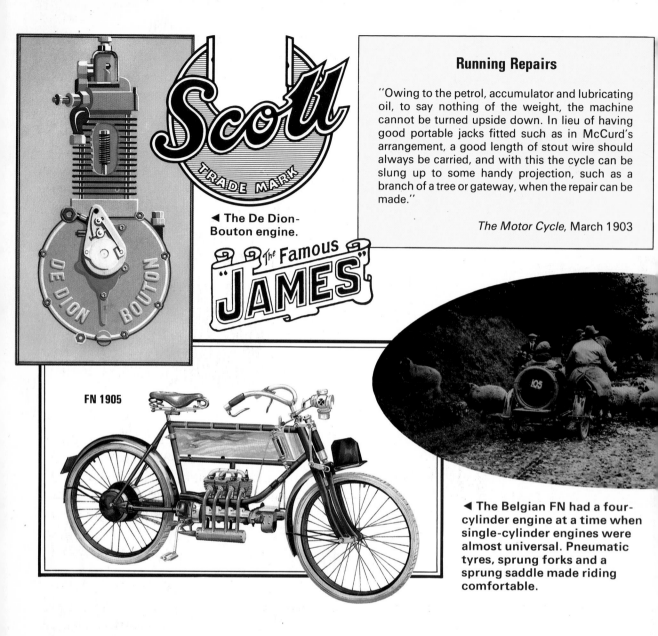

◄ The De Dion-Bouton engine.

FN 1905

◄ The Belgian FN had a four-cylinder engine at a time when single-cylinder engines were almost universal. Pneumatic tyres, sprung forks and a sprung saddle made riding comfortable.

Many bicycle manufacturers decided to add engines to their vehicles. Small cyclomotor attachments were built in Switzerland, France and Belgium. Britain had to import engines, mainly from France, where Compte Albert de Dion and Georges Bouton started making engines in 1895. The De Dion-Bouton engine, along with other proprietary engines such as the Belgian Minerva, the Swiss Motosacoche and the German Fafnir were snapped up by British motorcycle manufacturers to found marques such as Ariel, Matchless, Triumph, Royal Enfield and Norton.

In 1901, the Werner Brothers, two Russians working in Paris, moved the Dion-Bouton engine on their cycles from over the front wheel to the bottom of the frame in place of the pedalling gear. The new layout worked so well from the mechanical point of view that other manufacturers copied the idea. Every bike on sale today has the engine in the same position as the 1901 Werner.

Road trials, hill climbs and road racing, which began in Austria and Germany in 1899, all helped manufacturers to improve their models. In 1903, the German Bosch company produced the first high tension magneto; in

► A 1914 Sunbeam advertisement emphasizes the sporting success of the machine.

▼ Rutted, unsurfaced roads were not the only hazard in the early days of motorcycling! The 1911 American Indian (below) shocked the British public when it beat a Matchless at a special race at Brooklands.

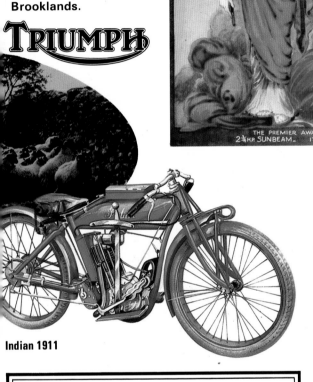

Indian 1911

THE PREMIER AWARD IN THE 1913 ENGLISH SIX DAYS A.C.U. RELIABILITY TRIALS WENT TO A 2¾ H.P. SUNBEAM. IT BEAT ALL OTHER MOTOR CYCLES IRRESPECTIVE OF CLASS AND HORSE POWER.

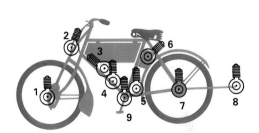

Engine Positions

Early motorcycle manufacturers placed the engine in a variety of positions. The Werner Brothers finally placed it centrally in 1901.

1 Singer 2 Werner 1899 3 Phelon & Moore 4 Laurin & Klement 5 Beeston 6 Ormonde 7 Millet 8 Humber 9 Werner 1901

1909, Scott introduced their all chain-drive kick starter. When Zenith introduced a multi-speed system on their Gradua they won so many events that the newly formed Auto Cycle Union of Britain barred them from racing. The Zenith company were delighted and began using a new trade mark featuring the word 'Barred'.

By 1912 engine sizes had grown to 500 cc and more and speeds had risen accordingly. Some of the fastest machines could reach 130 km/h (80 mph). Two and three speed gear boxes were becoming common and ignition systems had improved enormously.

In 1911 the famous Tourist Trophy races, testing ground for dozens of new models every year, were held for the fifth time on the Isle of Man. The first three places in the Senior race were taken by the American Indian, with its sophisticated vee engine. Together with the Harley Davidson bikes which had first been produced as early as 1903, the new vee engines became increasingly popular. By 1914, motor-cycling had become an enjoyable, practical type of transport.

The Golden Years

During the First World War, motorcycle industries began producing machines for military use. Clyno in Britain won a government contract to build sidecar outfits fitted with heavy Vickers machine guns. These were used to equip the first military units made up entirely of motorcycles. Douglas, Triumph and Phelon and Moore all produced solo despatch rider bikes. The Triumph in particular was so dependable that servicemen named it the 'Trusty'. In Germany, a wide variety of machines was used. A new company was set up – BMW, later to become famous for its motorcycles.

After the war there was a huge demand for bikes. By 1920 more than 100 new firms had sprung up in Britain alone. Many of the new models were technically advanced but, because they had not been properly tested, they proved to be unreliable. Sopwith, famous for their Sopwith Camel fighter aircraft, developed the ABC in 1919; in spite of some fine racing successes it proved unreliable and production stopped. The enormous demand for bikes caused prices to rocket. This did not stop the boom from spreading. The Golden Years of motorcycling had begun.

In Italy the first Moto Guzzis appeared in 1921. They featured rear springing. In Germany the first 500 cc flat twin BMW bikes appeared in 1923. In a much developed 1000 cc form, the BMW is still popular today. In Britain many riders wanted superbikes, like the 600 cc overhead camshaft Square Four

The 1930 Matchless Silver Hawk was one of the most advanced models of its day. With its overhead camshaft, transverse vee four engine, cantilever suspension and coil ignition, it seems more like a modern superbike than a 60-year old veteran.

Matchless Silver Hawk 1930

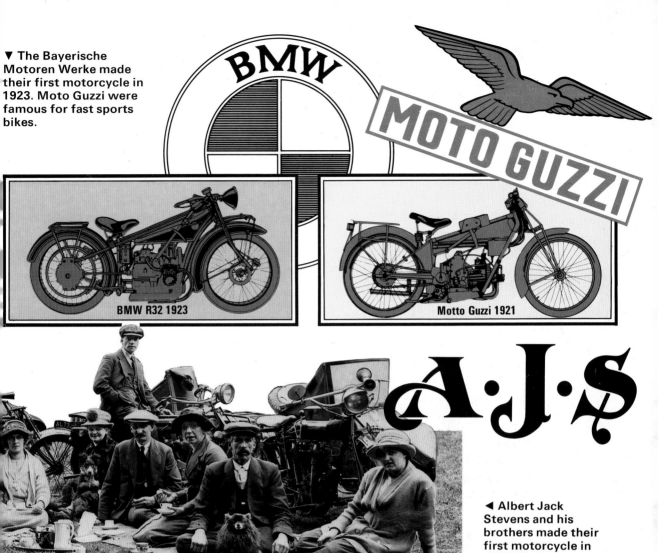

▼ The Bayerische Motoren Werke made their first motorcycle in 1923. Moto Guzzi were famous for fast sports bikes.

BMW R32 1923

Motto Guzzi 1921

◄ Albert Jack Stevens and his brothers made their first motorcycle in 1897. The initials AJS were used on their machines from 1909.

Ariel and the transverse vee-four Matchless Silver Hawk. Few could afford them.

The greatest demand was for small, cheap motorcycles. France, Italy, Switzerland, and Austria all produced cheap lightweight motorcycles and mopeds, leaving much of the luxury bike market to British firms like Brough Superior, Norton, AJS and Velocette.

Many firms took their racing activities very seriously, and the TTs of the 1920s saw bitterly fought duels. But by the 1930s Norton's new 500 cc overhead camshaft single CS1 had the 500 cc Senior race sewn up, while the Velocette KTT range had tremendous success in the 350 cc Junior TT race.

At the same time some exciting early superbikes were being developed. At the 1928 Earls Court Show three manufacturers – AJW, McEvoy and Brough – launched four-cylinder models. One famous Brough enthusiast was Lawrence of Arabia.

Bikes had not only improved mechanically by the 1930s. They had begun to look much more like the machines we are familiar with today. Chrome plating was first used in America to brighten up Harley Davidson and Indian vee twins and four-cylinder Hendersons. The familiar 'saddle' shape of petrol tank replaced the old box-shaped 'flat tank' and, by the middle of the decade, foot-operated gear changes and electric lighting were common features.

By the 1920s, the 'commuter market' had developed. People who would never have considered riding a bike bought lightweights just to go to work on. The bigger manufacturers were able to build and sell a much wider range because of this. BSA in Britain offered everything from a 150 cc single up to a 1000 cc vee twin all through the 1930s.

One of the greatest models from a great marque, the Norton 500 cc overhead camshaft of 1927 was the first in a line of racing machinery that kept Norton at the forefront of the racing world. Overhead camshaft Nortons won 14 out of a possible 16 TTs between 1931 and 1938. Road-going versions of their racers, sometimes called 'TT replicas' helped Norton become one of the world's most successful manufacturers.

Norton CS1 1927

▲ **Riders line up at the Brooklands circuit in 1925. Brooklands was the leading purpose-built circuit in Britain in the 1920s, the scene of marathons and record attempts as well as races.**

In 1933 Triumph launched a 650 cc vertical twin that proved itself by covering 500 miles in as many minutes. Just five years later another vertical twin Triumph, the 500 cc Speed Twin, appeared. It was to alter the whole pattern of the British industry. But once again the world went to war and motorcycle manufacturers turned to military production.

Bikes were not often used as weapon-carrying vehicles but they were vital for carrying dispatches. Harley Davidson and Indian built more than 300,000 bikes for the American forces. Japan built replica Harley Davidsons. They were almost all 750 cc and 500 cc vee twins. Germany relied mostly on BMW flat twins and Zandupp flat fours.

Having occupied Belgium, Germany took over the FN factory where the Gnome Rhone sidecar outfit was being developed, complete with sidecar drive. They adapted it for their BMWs and Zandupps. Carrying a three-man crew, heavy machine-gun on the sidecar and full equipment, one of the German outfits could go into action carrying more than three quarters of a ton and still accelerate up to 85 km/h (55 mph). Used in all motorcycle units the outfits became devastating weapons in Germany's 'blitzkrieg' method of mechanized warfare.

Italy depended on Gileras and the 500 cc Moto Guzzi. Britain used 350 cc and 500 cc single-cylinder models from BSA, Norton, Triumph, Matchless, Ariel and Velocette and 125 cc James and Royal Enfield two-strokes. Matchless used a new type of telescopic fork called 'Teledraulic', which was later adopted throughout the industry.

The name Velocette was originally used as a model name for a lightweight two-stroke made by the Veloce company. During the 1920s and the late 1930s, overhead camshaft models beat all comers. After the Second World War Velocette's reputation was founded on 350 cc and 500 cc overhead valve single-cylinder road bikes, including the Viper, Venom and Thuxton.

By the end of the war in 1945 the motorcycling industry had changed radically. Bikes had become neater, cleaner, quieter and more powerful. Following Triumph's vertical twins, BSA soon produced its 'A' series and Norton the Dominator 88 and 99. As in the 1920s and 1930s, British bikes dominated the market, but the Golden Years of motorcycling had come to an end. More and more people began to buy cars. But in Tokyo a small factory started making a few lightweight motorcycles. A new era of motorcycling was about to begin. The factory was run by a man called Honda.

Velocette

▼ **Puch have been making a huge variety of bikes since 1903.**

▲ **To many, MV Augusta's high-performance roadsters were among the ultimate superbikes.**

The name Vincent is best known for the 1000 cc overhead valve vee twins that were among the most exciting machines ever produced in Britain. In its standard form it was known as the Rapide and had a top speed of over 160 km/h (110 mph) as long ago as 1948. The performance of the Black Shadow was such that road-testers were unable to give an accurate top speed, but it was certainly in excess of 190 km/h (120 mph).

VINCENT

The Fifties

Triumph had gained a lead on the rest of the British industry in 1937 by introducing the revolutionary Speed Twin. After the Second World War, riders excited by the performance of the Triumph, demanded more of the same, and in the space of a few years BSA, Norton, Ariel, Matchless, AJS and Royal Enfield all built vertical twins.

Triumph now boosted the Speed Twin's 500 cc engine to 650 cc and called the new model the Thunderbird. Other manufacturers followed and the 650 vertical twin became the hallmark of the British industry in the 1950s.

In the racing world, British single-cylinder machines were now outclassed by multi-cylinder Italian models. The Italians produced some sophisticated racers that even the best Norton and AJS singles could not compete with.

While most European countries improved their lightweight motorcycle, moped and scooter industries, exports of British lightweight machines fell. British riders began to buy imported lightweights, especially scooters. Most British manufacturers continued to concentrate on big bikes, like the Vincent 1000 cc vee twin, which never sold in large numbers. In the late 1950s the Japanese industry turned its attention to the European market.

▲ Jeff Smith, a top BSA rider.
▼ Geoff Duke won a string of championships in the 1950s.

▼ Mike Hailwood, known as 'Mike the Bike' won Honda their first World Championship in 1961. Between 1963 and 1967 he won nine World Championships and eleven TT races.

Japanese Manufacturers

Honda, the best established Japanese manufacturer, was set up in 1948. The first Suzuki was made in 1952, the first Yamaha in 1954, and the name Kawasaki first appeared on a petrol tank in 1961. The first world beating Japanese bike was the 50 cc Honda Super Club. Over 24,000 were made in its first year. By 1965, 15 years after Honda produced their first bike, Japanese motorcycle production had passed two million each year. About a quarter of these machines were exported.

Honda, the biggest motorcycle manufacturers in the world, could hardly have had a more humble beginning. Soichiro Honda bought a small batch of stationary engines in 1946

▼ In 1975, the Honda Gold Wing became the first Japanese touring bike.

Honda Gold Wing

The 250 cc Honda CB250N is an example of lightweight design. Although not designed to be a particularly fast model, the tidy motor will propel the bike comfortably at around 145 km/h (90 mph).

and employed a dozen workers to fit them into bicycle frames. There was so little petrol in postwar Japan that he had to adapt them to run on a spirit distilled from pine trees! Within three years the first complete Honda bike appeared, the two-stroke single-cylinder *Dream*. In 1961 Honda won the 125 cc and 250 cc World Championships and by 1962 had made more than a million bikes.

During the 1960s Suzuki, Yamaha and Kawasaki also started sending bikes to America and Europe. At first they sold only lightweights. By the end of the 1960s the British industry was in trouble. American Harley Davidsons, German BMWs and Italian Moto Guzzis and Ducatis were not made in large enough numbers to satisfy demand. Unsurprisingly, when Honda introduced the first CB750 four-cylinder model in 1968, Japan started to take over the big bike market.

How it Works

The basic concept of the motorcycle has not changed much in almost ninety years. Some of the early pioneers had four-cylinder, four-stroke engines, suspension, brakes and lighting. But how they would have envied today's motorcyclists. Undamped, poorly sprung forks have been replaced by hydraulically damped units at front and rear. Powerful discs have replaced unreliable bicycle type brakes. Carefully designed, efficient carburettors and electronic 'pointless' ignition enable a modern bike to run better than would ever have been thought possible. Early four-stroke engines featured 'automatic' valves that were merely one-way trap doors that let gas in and out of an engine haphazardly. Valve timing on a modern engine is controlled precisely – another reason for the amazing performance of many of today's bikes.

Because a two-stroke has fewer moving parts than a four-stroke engine, there is less to go wrong with it.

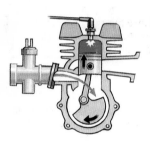

▲ As the piston moves up, the fuel mixture is sucked into the crankcase. At the same time, the mixture sucked in on the previous stroke is exploded above the piston.

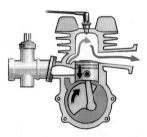

▲ As the piston is forced down the barrel, gases escape through the exhaust port, and the cycle starts again.

A Headlight		
B Fork spring	D Stainless steel disc	F Hydraulic flu reservoir
C Hydraulic disc brake caliper	E Speedometer/ Tachometer	G Indicator

The diagram shows what makes a modern motorcycle come to life. Air is being sucked into the carburettor (1) through the air filter that keeps dust and grit out of the engine. Mixed with petrol and ignited by a spark plug in the combustion chamber (2), it explodes and forces the piston down the cylinder. The movement of the piston turns the crankshaft, and this turning movement passes through the gears (3) to the rear wheel by the primary drive and the rear chain. Waste gas from the engine escapes through the exhaust pipe.

The engine spins at around 10,000 rpm and it has a top speed of 160 km/h (100 mph). It is stopped by a hydraulic disc brake and is hydraulically sprung at front and rear.

Rear view mirror

Passenger grab rail   K Rear suspension unit   M Air filter   O Piston

Rear/stop light   L Silencer baffle   N Wet multi plate clutch P Speedometer cable

                                                                                   Q Oil level check window

                                                                                   R Rear brake cable

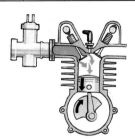

INDUCTION: Inlet valve open, piston moving down to suck in a mixture of air and petrol.

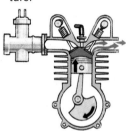

COMPRESSION: The spinning crankshaft sends the piston back up to compress the mixture.

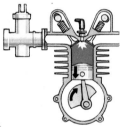

POWER: The spark explodes the mixture, forcing the piston down to turn the crankshaft.

EXHAUST: Exhaust valve open, the piston expels waste gases before repeating cycle.

Birth of a Bike

The process starts with the idea. Honda, for example, might decide that a six-cylinder 1000 cc superbike is what they need as a new top of the range model. A research and development team takes that idea and produces detailed plans. They have to bear in mind the cost of all the components as the finished product has to be sold in a competitive market.

Once the engine and transmission has been designed the correct type of frame and suspension has to be chosen and a prototype i built by hand. A factory road tester takes th bike out on a special track where it is tested t its limit. Any faults are then corrected. A pric is calculated. After all this preparation, a efficient production line is set up, and Honda' idea for a six-cylinder dream bike materialize in the classic CBX.

e Suzuki GS750 engine
oduces a maximum 68
rsepower and will push
e Suzuki along at 200 km/h
25 mph).

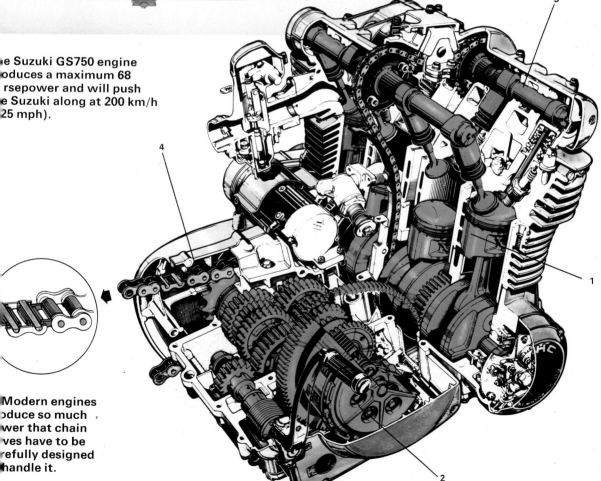

Modern engines
oduce so much
wer that chain
ves have to be
refully designed
handle it.

Road Racing

Early races were easily organized. A group of riders would simply agree on a course and roar off at top speed on local public roads. Not

▼ Randy Mamola's speed into a corner is captured in this spectacular picture taken at the 1984 Belgian Grand Prix (left). Stunt rider Dave Taylor takes a circuit on one wheel (right).

▼ Randy Mamola's speed into a corner is captured in this spectacular picture taken at the 1984 Belgian Grand Prix (left). Stunt rider Dave Taylor takes a circuit on one wheel (right).

surprisingly racing was unpopular with the public who were none too keen on the idea of intrepid young riders roaring down the high street, and racing was declared illegal in some countries. On the Continent some authorities took a sympathetic view of the new sport, and for the first few years of this century long-distance races between towns such as Paris and Madrid and Paris and Vienna were particularly popular.

To get round the ban on road racing in Britain the Autocycle Club organized road races on the Isle of Man, where riders could compete for the Tourist Trophy. British riders wanted to race more than once a year. They could not race on the road but there was no law against racing on purpose-built tracks.

In 1908 a concrete banked race track was built at Brooklands in the south of England. It was to become the scene of many epic contests

and dramatic record-breaking rides. Although the sport is still known as 'road racing' races are nowadays almost invariably held well away from public roads.

As road racing developed competition between various marques intensified. Racing bikes were no longer just highly tuned roadsters.

Beacuse of the prestige attached to a successful racing programme and the resulting increase in sales of the ordinary machines manufacturers spent alot of money on building a handful of special racers.

By the early 1920s British factories had well established, successful racing teams. Although the annual pilgrimage to the Isle of Man TT was the most important event, they were eager to take on their rivals, and there was no shortage of French, Belgian, German and Italian teams ready to meet them.

Strong opposition came from advanced models like the French 500 cc dohc vertical twin Peugeot, Italian ohc Bianchis and Moto-Guzzis, and what was to become the most formidable racer of all, the BMW. At first Norton, AJS and Velocette ohc big singles dominated world championships. But by the late 1950s Italian bikes began to dominate the circuits.

Racing Machines

Although production racing bikes have to be based on standard road models, top class racers have little in common with 'road legal' machines. Over the years, designers have found that they could build engines to go fast, but at the expense of engine life. Today, no one expects a competitive racing engine to last more than one season, and a two- or three-year-old racer cannot compete against a brand new bike. Gearing, suspension and tyres are all crucial to a rider's performance, and machines are designed so that adjustments can be made in the pits as quickly as possible.

Solo riders lean their bikes over at alarming angles when cornering: Mick Grant on his Kawasaki (above left) and Eddie Lawson (above) show how it should be done. Sidecar passengers use their body weight to keep their outfits stable (left).

Using relatively cheap machines to gain experience, racing stars began to make their names. While such riders as Percy Tait and Phil Read were winning their first races, the Italian marques, notably MV Augusta, were having astonishing success. Every solo class of the 1956 TT was won by an Italian machine.

In 1959 Honda entered their first TT. They were followed by Suzuki, Yamaha and Kawasaki until all but the 80 cc and 125 cc classes were dominated by Japanese machines. Riding for Honda, American Freddie Spencer became the first man ever to take both the 500 cc and 250 cc World Championships in the same season in 1985. In 1984 the 500 cc honours went to Yamaha; in 1983 it was Honda and in 1982 Suzuki.

Many countries hold their own national championships, and the FIM (*Fédération Internationale Motocycliste*) organize world championships for 125 cc, 250 cc and 500 cc solo machines, and for racing sidecar outfits. Most would-be champions start at club level where cheaper machines can still be competitive. A 'privateer' who proves himself at amateur level might find a local business to sponsor him. He will almost certainly aspire to join the elite of works riders. Contesting the world championships at various rounds across the globe is an exciting dream for a newcomer.

Whether a field of amateur riders are competing in a local club race or top stars are battling for the world championship, road racing involves an element of danger. No rider is allowed to race without wearing a protective leather suit, gloves, boots and, of course, a crash helmet. The machines are also checked by 'scrutineers' before each race to see that they are not leaking oil that could cause crashes, while straw bales and carefully designed barriers help to minimize the outcome of any accident.

▲ Left: British veteran Phil
Read won two World
Championships for Yamaha in
the mid-1960s, before moving
to MV Augusta to take the 1973
and 1974 500 cc
championships.
Right: 1985 double World
Champion Freddie Spencer
celebrates victory in the
premier American motorcycle
event, the Daytona Formula 1
Grand Prix. Spencer took the
world titles in the 250 cc and
500 cc classes.

◄ One of the greatest road
racing stars of all time, Italian
Giacomo Agostini in action at
the Dutch TT (left). His record
included ten Isle of Man TT
victories and fifteen World
Championships.
Rivals Freddie Spencer and
Eddie Lawson look each other
over before the start of the
1984 Austrian Grand Prix
(right).

Speedway

Speedway is easily the most popular motorcycling spectator sport. It has a flourishing league system like football, complete with championships, transfers and supporters' clubs. Many large towns in Europe have a speedway circuit, yet speedway was invented in America, developed in Australia, and only began in Britain in 1928.

Speedway bikes are among the most specialized of all. Modern ones are all 500 cc single-cylinder models. The British Godden firm produces a successful model. The 1989 champion Hans Nielsen rides a Godden machine. A tiny tank holds enough fuel for four laps of a 400 metre circuit. Most bikes have only one gear and none of them is fitted with any form of brake!

Racing is usually fast and furious in a speedway league match, because there are thirteen heats in an evening with two riders from each team riding in each race. In a seven-man team there are three 'heat leaders', two 'second strings' and two 'reserves'. Normally the heat leaders and second strings have four rides each and the reserves three.

The surface of the track is a layer of loose shale laid over hardcore, and it is carefully watered and rolled. Each rider scores three points for a win, two for a second and one for a third. Instead of riding round the bends of the course in the normal way, the riders 'broadside' their bikes around the corners. A rider's steel-shod left boot scrapes through the shale, and the dirt showers everywhere as he careers around the floodlit track.

Three other speedway-like sports are also popular. Grass track racing is carried out on a field in daylight instead of a prepared track under floodlights. Unlike speedway, sidecars also take part. Sand racing is the only motorcycling sport to be held on a beach.

For many people, especially in Eastern Europe and Scandinavia, the most exciting form of speedway is ice racing. As the name implies, the circuit is of solid ice, so there is no grip even for special speedway tyres. To overcome this steel spikes are fixed to the tyre to grip the ice. So good is the grip given by these spikes that bikes can take corners when they are lying almost flat. A roadracer has reinforced knees on his leathers for cornering. An ice racer has reinforced elbows!

▲ Needle-sharp spikes attached to the rear tyre of an ice racer ensure grip on the track. The rider wears heavy leg protection (above). Dust flies as bikes slide round a corner in a conventional speedway race during the 1978 World Team Cup (below).

▶ Speedway has its own special techniques, machines and clothing. In these pictures of Michael Lee and Rudy Muts, steel-shod legs are extended to balance their bikes around a bend. Riders rely on a skilful combination of speed and balance to get around quickly and safely.

The Collins Family

Peter, Phil, Leslie and Neil Collins could be called the first family of speedway. Peter is the only rider to have scored maximum points in three consecutive World Team Cups. Peter, Phil and Leslie are all former Junior speedway champions, an achievement unequalled by any other family. Peter has twice ridden to victory in the World Pairs Championship, partnered in 1983 by Kenny Carter and in 1984 by Chris Morton.

Michael Lee

No other rider has made the same impact on world class speedway as British star Michael Lee. In his first three years as a professional, he won the British Championship twice, and came a creditable fourth in the 1977 World Championships in Gothenburg in Sweden. In 1980 he won the World Championship and in 1981 the World Longtrack Championship.

Ivan Mauger

Ivan Mauger is the grand old man of professional speedway. The veteran New Zealander has won five World Championships, including a unique hat trick of three consecutive wins between 1968 and 1970. He also won three longtrack World Championships in 1971, 1972 and 1976. While nearing the end of an illustrious career, Mauger organized a series of 'all star' matches to end his time on the shale in style.

Motocross

Cross country racing dates back more than fifty years, but the sport really took off in its present form after the Second World War. Factory sponsored riders rode BSA, Norton, Matchless, AJS and Ariels in Britain. Competitors rode Husqvarna in Sweden and FN in Belgium. They were powerful but by modern standards were ridiculously overweight, so scrambling, as the sport used to be called, was not nearly so exciting as it is today.

The big 500 cc class of motorcross racing was in danger of stagnating in the late 1950s, but in the lightweight 250 cc class a revolution was taking place. Highly tuned 250 cc two-strokes built by Husqvarna, CZ in Czechoslovakia and Greeves in Britain soon dominated the 250 cc class. They began to enter 500 cc races and often beat the bigger bikes. New rules stopped this, so factories that built the new type of quick 250 built bigger versions.

There is a huge demand for motocross machines. Suzuki invested a large amount of time and money developing the most expensive motocross bikes ever raced. Their efforts paid off, and they won the 250 cc motocross world championship at their first attempt. Top line machines are now built by Suzuki, Honda, Yamaha, and Kawasaki as well as by European factories such as Cagiva, Husqvarna and KTM. Championships are held for 125, 250 and 500 cc classes, with more than 40 championship events around the world. Bikes have become so highly tuned that most factories concentrate on making them handle better. This is of critical importance as with better suspension the rider can keep the bike on the ground for more of the race, rather than spend his time making impressive but time-consuming jumps.

Sidecar motocross, sometimes called 'sidecar cross' is every bit as exciting as solo motocross. Most outfits are powered either by purpose-built engines from experts such as EML, or modified solo motocross engines.

Like any all-action sport, motocross can be dangerous. When a bike is ridden hard over rough ground its rear wheel picks up stones and throws them out like bullets. To protect themselves, riders wear lightweight plastic 'armour' and face guards as well as helmets and padded leather suits. Many also wear wide body belts to help them withstand the shock of landing after a jump.

► British champion Graham Noyce demonstrates the kind of skill that put him at the top of his sport. He is as much at home in the air as on the ground!

▲ Motocross action: the 'Flying Finn' Heikki Mikkola takes off at the top of a steep climb at the British Grand Prix. The crowds in the background give some idea of the popularity of the sport.

Graham Noyce, the golden boy of British motocross, became so successful that, like many film stars, he lived abroad to avoid paying too much tax! Graham started riding in schoolboy scrambles, and rode a West German Maico during his first full seasons as a professional in 1976 and 1977. He won the British Championship in both years, and joined Honda as a works rider before going on to win twice more in 1978 and 1979. In 1979 he added the 500 cc world title to his honours. A leg injury in 1983 led to his eventual retirement from a sport that requires a high degree of physical fitness. He is now back in Britain, and reputed to be a millionaire, thanks to his great success in the sport.

▲ This kind of close racing is what motocross is all about. Mud and stones fly at the start of a race in the Netherlands (left), and riders battle round a corner at a British meeting (right). A rider tackles a water splash (above right).

Schoolboy Scrambling

The fact that Motocross is one of the toughest sports around has not stopped young riders trying to compete and make a success of it. What started as a novelty has developed into Schoolboy Scrambling, tightly organized and hard fought. Youngsters start competing as soon as they are old enough to go to school. They wear the same protective clothing as the professionals, and take the same risks. Special lightweight 50 cc and 80 cc machines are available. Some clubs run their own schoolboy sections, but many newcomers prefer to join a specialist club.

Trials

Road racers, sprinters and speedway riders all compete on specially prepared tracks. Even a rugged motocross course is generally carefully laid out for an event. But for a trial, organizers go out of their way to find the most hazardous natural courses possible – rocky stream beds, loose gravel, exposed tree roots, mud wallows and rough countryside that would be tough to walk over. Trials riders attempt to ride their bikes through these hazards.

A course is divided into a number of sections with an observer at each section. At the start of the event competitors are given 'route charts' with instructions on how to reach the observed sections and score cards to be marked by observers before continuing. Arriving at a section, riders may have to wait for earlier arrivals to ride through it. They use this time to walk through the section and give each other advice. This may sound odd in a competitive sport, but trial riders compete against the course, not against each other.

From the moment a competitor rides past the 'section starts' sign until he leaves the section, the observer watches his every move. If he looses his balance and puts a foot down to keep going the observer puts one mark on his card. For two or three of these 'dabs' the rider gets a corresponding number of penalty points; if he stops, falls off, or wanders outside the marked route, he incurs the maximum five points. At the end of the event the rider with the lowest number of points wins.

The first trial bikes were almost identical to ordinary roadsters. Over the years they have evolved into models designed specifically for rough country. In the 1950s Ariel, AJS and Matchless 350 cc models were popular as they had the slogging power to cope with the adverse conditions. Although they had knobbly tyres for maximum grip, high level exhaust pipes less liable to damage from rocks, and small petrol tanks, they were still based on road-going bikes. Ultra-light two-strokes have replaced them. British two-strokes such as Greeves, DOT and Cotton showed riders that a small engine of around 250 cc was powerful enough for the job. Later Spanish bikes – Ossas Bultacos and Montesas – took over. Beta and Fantic are also among the manufacturers of trial bikes. They have high ground clearance and metal guards under the frame to protect the engine from damage. They are the lightest of all sporting bikes.

Enduros

The two most famous Enduros, the Scottish Six Days Trial and the International Six Day Enduro have their roots back in early reliability trials. Intended to test machine and rider to the limit, the International Six Day Enduro calls for riders to cover many miles of very rough countryside on machines that can be given no more than the bare minimum of maintenance during the contest. Riders carry a tool kit and have to do all their own repairs, so an Enduro rider must be a skilled mechanic as well as a skilled motocross rider with some skill at trials. During the course of an Enduro, riders have to make their way across rough countryside while keeping to a set time schedule. Any repairs must be made during that time. Special timed sections also help establish a winner.

▲ Trials champions going through their paces. Finn Yrio Vesterinen at the Scottish Six Days Trial (left). Yorkshireman Martin Lampkin demonstrates the art of balancing the bike with the weight of his body on a rocky climb (centre). Mick Andrews takes a dab at the Hurst Cup Trial (right).

◄ The maestro, Irishman Sammy Miller, on his famous 500 cc Ariel

ISDE Trophies

The ISDE Trophy has been offered to six-man teams since 1913, and the Vase to four-man teams since 1924.

	Trophy	Vase
1982	Czech	E. Germany
1983	Sweden	Sweden
1984	Netherlands	E. Germany
1985	Sweden	E. Germany
1986	Italy	Italy
1987	E. Germany	E. Germany
1988	France	Italy
1989	Italy	England

Famous Circuits

TT Champions

1979	Phil Read
1980	Mike Hailwood
1981	Ron Haslam
1982	Joey Dunlop
1983	Joey Dunlop
1984	Joey Dunlop
1985	Joey Dunlop
1986	Joey Dunlop
1987	Virginio Ferrari
1988	Carl Fogarty
1989	Carl Fogarty

ISLE OF MAN

As any motorcycle fan will confirm, there is no circuit in the world to compare with the 'Mountain Circuit' on the Isle of Man. The 61-km course is made up entirely of ordinary roads in the old tradition of the sport, and during the course of a six-lap race both rider and machine face the ultimate test of endurance.

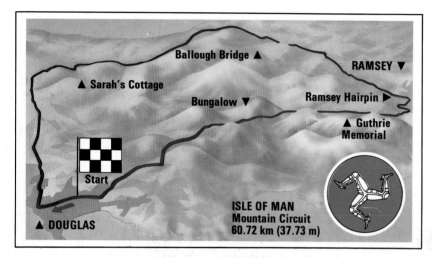

ISLE OF MAN
Mountain Circuit
60.72 km (37.73 m)

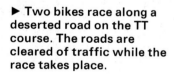

► Two bikes race along a deserted road on the TT course. The roads are cleared of traffic while the race takes place.

British riders first used the Isle of Man in 1905 as a practice ground for the great continental 'Coupes International' road races. Then in 1907 a race was organized for touring machines. Eager to act as hosts to the Tourist Trophy races, the Isle of Man authorities closed off 24 kilometres (16 miles) of road for the first races. Charlie Collier won the single cylinder class on a Matchless, while a Norton ridden by Rex Fowler won the twin cylinder class. In 1911 the course was extended to the Mountain Course so beloved by TT fans, and the circuit was last changed in 1920.

▲ The late Mike Hailwood returned to the TT after an 11-year absence to win the 1978 trophy – much to the delight of his many fans around the course. A feature of the TT circuit is the variety of conditions a rider encounters. They can be basking in hot sunshine on the lower sections, then battling through mist and rain in the mountain sections.

BRANDS HATCH

Brands Hatch is certainly the best known road racing circuit in Britain and it was one of the first modern British road racing circuits. Brands Hatch is a circuit with a grasstrack history, like Mallory Park. Local grasstrackers from the two circuits used to meet for challenge meetings in the 1950s. As the airfield circuits which had been used for club racing in the immediate post-war period began to deteriorate, Brands Hatch and Mallory Park were both given a tarmac coating to become two of the first modern circuits.

Bikes at Brands

Sadly, attendance at road race meetings has declined in recent years, but Brands Hatch, like other British circuits, has been playing host to a variety of other events. In 1989 the Classic Racing Motorcycle Club attracted over 25,000 spectators to their Superprix meeting at the Kent circuit.

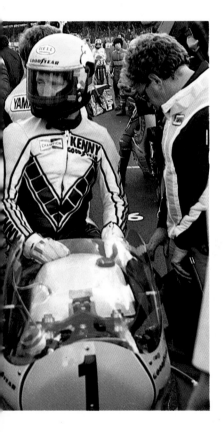

▲ American Kenny Roberts enjoyed neck and neck rivalry with British ace Barry Sheene. He took the world 500 cc title back to the United States in 1978 – the first American to win the trophy. He retained it in 1979 and 1980.
Close cornering at a 1984 World Championship event: Eddie Lawson leads Freddie Spencer (right).

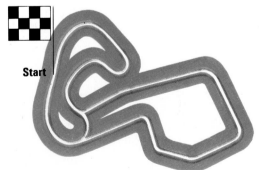

Start

BRANDS HATCH
Grand Prix Circuit
4.26 km (2.65 m)

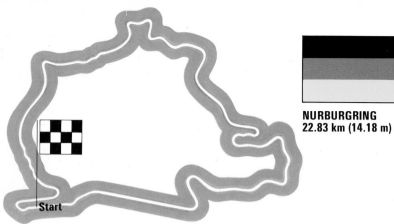

▶ The start of a Belgian sidecar Grand Prix in 1978.

▼ Giacomo Agostini has won on every major circuit in Europe (centre). Angel Nietro specialized in the lightweight 50 cc and 125 cc classes (left). Joey Dunlop (right) won the Isle of Man TT in 1980 and again in 1985.

NURBURGRING

The German Nurburgring course is one of the best-known circuits in Europe. More than 22 km (13 miles) long, running partly through pine forests and with some vicious curves, the Nurburgring has been criticized for having a poor standard of rider safety. This is partly due to the number of Armco crash barriers, which can do more harm than good in the event of a crash. Like the Isle of Man, the Nurburgring remains a great centre for motocyclists from all over the world. The old Nurburgring is still in use, but has been joined by a purpose-built 4.5 kilometre (3.5 miles) track just next door with more modern facilities.

LE MANS
Circuit Bugatti
4.24 km (2.63 m)

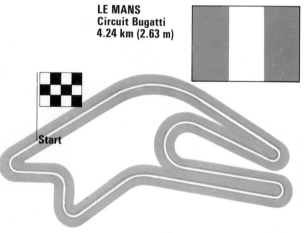

LE MANS

To many road racing fans the Le Mans circuit still represents all that is best in Continental racing. Today Le Mans is used even more for bike racing than for cars. It is a classic example of a short 'scratching' circuit; a mixture of hair-pin bends and fast straights that stretch riders' skill to the limit.

Start

ASSEN
Circuit Van Drenthe
6.13 km (3.81 m)

ASSEN
Even the best riders find the van Drenthe circuit challenging. At the Dutch TT top racers compete in yet another round of the World Championships, and in the FIM Formula One Championship. Following a fatal accident in 1975, the circuit was modified to include new tight right- and left- hand bends before the main start and finish straight. In 1984 a new shorter circuit was introduced.

31

Drag Racing

Marion Owens and his bike are well matched: the American drag racing star is a 17-stone (238lb) giant and his bike a 3500 cc twin-engined Harley Davidson.

Take two or even three highly tuned, multicylinder high-performance engines. Squeeze then into a lightweight frame, supercharge them and feed them with potent nitro methane. Fit a wide 'slick' rear tyre to transmit all that power to the track. Now find a daring volunteer to try and hold this supercharged monster in a straight line as it rockets away to cover less than half a kilometre in under eight seconds, finishing up at over 290 km/h (180 mph). Imagine two of these projectiles scorching away together with an earsplitting howl. That is exactly what happens at a drag race. 'Sprinting' as it used to be known, started in the 1920s when individual riders took turns trying to cover a measured distance in the shortest possible time. To make the contest more exciting competitors took to racing in pairs and, as competition became fiercer, specialist drag bikes were developed that had virtually nothing in common with other forms of sporting bikes, let alone humble road bikes. Nowadays 'dragsters' are painstakingly set up and tuned to bursting point – all for a few seconds.

Custom Bikes

Many riders alter their bikes to look like racers. These 'café racers' are often very fast, but the looks are important too. Other riders make more radical changes, especially to the front of the bike. The best known type of custom bike is the chopper which, like the café racer, was originally built to go faster than standard vehicles.

The idea of the chopper originted in America. Back in the late 1950s Triumph 650 cc Bonnevilles were gaining popularity there and riders of the huge 1200 cc Harley Davidsons were furious to discover that the 'Limey Lightweights' were faster than their 'Hogs'.

Harley riders began to 'chop' excess weight from the big twins by removing any non-essential parts. Today 'chops' come in all shapes and sizes and special shows are held in Europe and America for proud owners to exhibit their masterpieces and compete for trophies. Three-wheeled trikes are also popular. These were once based on the Harley Davidson 'Servicecars' used by the American police but now they are often fitted with powerful vee eight car engines.

A good custom bike can take years to build, and the care put into them by loving owners ensures that the best of them are not just motorcycles – they're works of art.

◄ This chopper is based on a 1200 cc Harley Davidson. Long custom girder forks have replaced the standard units, the seat level has been lowered and the footrests and controls moved forward. The result is a light, fast machine.

──Daredevils──

Many motorcyclists compete in organized sport but others prefer to see how far they can push their machines, and themselves. American stuntrider Evel Knievel's speciality is finding out how far he can make a bike fly through the air. He boasts that he has broken every bone in his body in various stunts. Not content with jumping over lorries, he has attempted to hang on to his rocket-powered 'Skycycle' and blast over the Snake Canyon in Colorado. He did not make it and had to parachute to safety halfway across.

Some stuntriders work in teams. Team acts include mock accidents, leaps over lines of cars, and rides through tunnels of fire. Many of the tricks performed by display teams and stunt teams are very similar, but display teams concentrate more on co-ordination and close team work. Some are military teams, who are incredibly precise in their performances. Some involve 20 or more riders at once moving in formation.

Other riders work alone. But even stars like Evel Knievel and British daredevils Eddie Kidd and 'Golly' Goddard rely on a team of helpers to stage their stunts. There are other determined individuals who take off to ride a bike where no one else has ever done it before. In 1976 a Japanese rider loaded his 175 cc Yamaha trial bike with extra petrol and lots of water and set off across the arid wastes of the Sahara. He made the trip successfully, turned round, and made the trip back home!

No matter how tough the challenge, somewhere there is a motorcycling daredevil ready to accept it.

▶ One of the most skilful stunt riders in the world is British whizz-kid, Eddie Kidd. He came to fame jumping over buses, but has now broadened his activities to include stunts for films (above).

▶ Every one of the Imps display team (far right) is under 16 years old – but that does not stop them from performing stunts every bit as difficult or delicate as those performed by older riders. Some of the team are as young as seven.

34

The Imps

Many dramatic stunts and world record attempts have been carried out by manufacturers trying to win the prestigious Maudes Trophy. Given to the Auto Cycle Union by Mr George Pettyt in 1923, it has been presented by them for "The most meritorious performance for an ACU certified test by a manufacturer". Norton won the trophy in 1923 when a 490 cc overhead valve model was assembled from parts selected by an ACU engineer and ridden at Brooklands for 12 hours non-stop, breaking 18 world records. Recent winners have included BMW, for a seven-day run round the TT course, and Suzuki, for a round-Britain ride.

Modern Bikes

Many would-be motorcyclists simply spend as much as they can afford on the biggest, most powerful bike possible. This is a big mistake. The first thing to do when choosing a bike is to ask yourself what you intend to use the bike for. If you intend to commute a few kilometres to work or school, pick a lightweight of 125 cc or less. Besides being easier to learn to ride, it will warm up to the correct operating temperature more quickly, which means the engine will last longer. It will also use less petrol and be easier to ride in traffic.

For touring and rallying, a 250 cc machine is adequate, but most riders would prefer a medium weight bike of around 400 to 650 cc. Fitted with a fairing, panniers and correct luggage carrying equipment, it will carry a rider, passenger and their luggage very happily. These are the most popular bikes of all. Then there are the superbikes. With modern engine performance, no one needs all the power these beautiful monsters have on tap. But most motorcyclists dream of riding a modern 'top of the range' model.

The Yamaha RD350F has a twin-cylinder two-stroke engine, liquid cooling and a six-speed gear box. Braking is looked after by discs at front and rear, and the machine has a distinctive racing look.

Although many British twins were in the 650 cc range, the size has been less popular on modern machines. Kawasaki's GPZ600-RX was a smaller and cheaper alternative to their famous 1000 cc superbikes. Like the bigger bikes, the 600 had a transverse double overhead camshaft four-cylinder engine and six-speed transmission. A light-box section frame, disc brakes and electronic ignition contributed to this mid-1980s medium-weight machine.

Suzuki's TS125X was based on their highly successful professional motocross machines. It would cruise at 105km/h (65 mph), and was capable of handling fairly rough ground.

The British motorcycle industry has recently made a comeback, with famous names like Norton and Triumph producing new models of advanced design. Norton are the only manufacturers in the world to use a rotary engine in their bikes today, with their F1 sports bike based closely on the JPS Rotary Racers that won many races in Britain in 1989. Triumph launched a new range of more conventional bikes in 1990, with three- and four-cylinder watercooled engines of 750 up to 1200 cc. Both are selling well all round the world, but in much smaller quantities than the Japanese companies.

Honda's XBR500 was designed and styled with the British enthusiast in mind. The simple and efficient 500 cc engine is a four-stroke, single cylinder design, with four valves operated by a single overhead camshaft, and twin exhausts.

The 250 cc air-cooled two-stroke twin Benelli (above) is an example of an Italian-built machine of the early 1980s.

37

Superbikes

With its wide rear wheel, long forks and old-style 'Fatbob' tank, the 1340 cc Harley Davidson Lowrider is the nearest thing to a chopper on the market.

Kawasaki claimed that their new GPZ100RX was the world's fastest production streetbike in 1985, with a top speed of around 260 km/h (161 mph). The power was produced by a transverse four-cylinder unit and delivered through a six-speed gear box. A light frame and aerodynamic fairing contributed to the bike's performance. For those who prefer something a little smaller, Honda's VFR750F is based on a powerful vee four 750 cc engine which develops 105 horsepower.

maha's FJ1200 is an enlarged sion of their 1100 cc model. e superbike market is the scene fierce competition between ns looking to make their bikes bit more powerful.

The Suzuki GSX-R1100 is top of a range of race-bred sports machines. The sixteen-valve, four-cylinder oil-cooled engine is capable of pushing the bike at more than 240 km/h (150 mph).

The most exotic, and certainly the rarest superbike of all was the Dutch designed and German built Van Veen (left). Powered by a transverse twin-rotor rotary engine, the manufacturers described its capacity as 996 cc, but there is controversy over how the size of a rotary engine should be calculated, and for sporting purposes, the engine is calculated to be an incredible 1992 cc! It was tested at speeds of over 215 km/h (133 mph), and with higher gearing had a theoretical top speed of more than 240 km/h (150 mph).

Since they built their first 500 cc sidevalve model in 1923 BMW have concentrated on flat twins, with capacities up to 1000 cc (above). Although twin-cylinder models are still available, the Munich factory's main effort is now directed towards a new range of in-line engined models. These include the K100 range, capable of over 220 km/h (135 mph), and the three-cylinder K75 – lighter and almost as fast, and with exceptionally smooth handling.

Index

Acknowledgements

Photographs: Allsport: 12 *top, centre,* 19 *right, bottom,* 20 *top,* 20–1 *bottom,* 22 *top,* 23 *right,* 24 *bottom,* 25 *top left,* 26 *top,* 27 *top left, top right,* 28 *top right,* 29 *left,* 30 *bottom,* 31 *top,* 32, 35 *top right;* Benelli: 1, 37 *top right;* BMW: 39 *centre right;* Mary Evans Picture Library: 4 *bottom left;* Harley Davidson: 38 *top left;* L.F Harris (Rushden) Ltd: 37 *top left;* Honda UK Limited: 13, 37 *bottom,* 38 *centre;* Kawasaki Motors UK Limited: 36 *top right,* 38 *bottom left;* Mansell Collection: 4 *top;* Don Morley 18 *left,* 20/21, 21 *top,* 28 *left;* 29 *right,* 31 *bottom;* National Motor Museum: 5 *top,* 7 *top;* Radio Times Hulton Picture Library: 10 *top left,* 12 *bottom;* Suzuki Motor Company: 16 *bottom,* 17 *top,* 36 *bottom,* 38–9 *top;* Van Veen: 38–9 *bottom;* Yamaha Motor NV: 16 *top,* 36 *top left,* 39 *top right;* Zefa: 18 *right,* 20 *bottom left,* 21 *top,* 25 *top right.* All other photographs kindly supplied by *Motor Cycle Weekly.*

Picture Research: Jackie Cookson.